Coachin

MW00945795

Powerful And Effective Coaching Questions To Kickstart Personal Growth And Succes Now!

I. Madison

Free Bonus inside

2nd EDITION

Table of Contents

Introduction

Chances are you have heard of the Coaching Questions. Most people have. Unfortunately, the coaching questions many people think about are those that get students to memorize formulae and answers to academic questions. This is not what this book is about. Rather, it is about knowing how to formulate questions that help to extract information voluntarily from the person whose success you are working on as a coach. In this book you are going to learn that coaching is not confined to sports and academics. You are also going to learn the difference between a coach and a tutor, two terms that are often confused. Also in the heart of it, this book illustrates the different categories of questions and shows how each of those categories helps in the coaching process. For anyone who has never had a coach, after reading through this book, you will realize how precious it is to have one, and that coaching is actually an enjoyable and refreshing process that prepares you for improved performance.

Any coach reading this book will also find valuable information that will help to make their trainees feel at ease, thus being able to speak out without inhibitions. When the people you are coaching communicate freely with you, you are bound to see the positive results in their performance. Coaching is close to medicine in that you cannot prescribe apt medicine unless you get the correct information. Thus, the need to learn the art of framing coaching questions appropriately. This is precisely what this book is set to teach you; and this, in simple clear language, and with practical examples to boot. On your own, you can only perform up to a certain limit. And this is not for lack of will, but because there are many distractions emanating from your social life, your lifestyle, economic stress, and many other aspects, many of which are beyond your control. However, a skilled coach is able to keep you focused; helping you to treat all distractions the way a helmeted bike rider treats the passing wind; or the way you treat the buzz of a mosquito outside your mosquito net.

As a coach, it is time to modify the way you design your coaching questions and make friends out of the people you train, motivating them all the way to success. And for anyone who has been hesitant about coaching, this book will assure you that a good coach will make your sessions a blast and the results great. One thing you are going to discover as you read this book is that coaching plays a big role in a person's success no matter the field. And where you could have succeeded anyway, coaching hastens the process and makes it less bumpy.

You will see in this book how well coaching does in matters of finance; issues of health; and even in matters of spirituality. And you will be amazed to know that coaching is not just great for employees on the lower ranks or for struggling business people. Rather, it is a necessity for top executives too and great entrepreneurs as well. What actually cuts across all cadres of people is that coaching leaves you self aware, self confident and motivated.

Happy reading and best wishes for your coaching success!

Chapter 1:
What, exactly, is coaching?

Supposing you heard this:

1. During that period, he made me recite the multiplication tables such that I could even say them in reverse order. He also helped me in other subjects.

2. During that period, he got me to learn the multiplication tables; do the rest of my homework in time; ensure my uniform is ready to wear come morning; and go to bed not later than 10pm every day.

Which of the above two would you call coaching, and which one would you call tutoring?

Wow! We usually do not give much thought to these things, do we? Let us say, when it comes to tutoring, it is more concentrated on teaching facts and the how-to things; sometimes getting to drilling. But when it comes to coaching, it is an all-round business. Your coach wants to help you set the right environment for working or for doing whatever else is in question, even as you get assistance in gaining knowledge and skills.

So clearly, number 1 above is about tutoring, while number 2 is geared towards coaching.

Is that why sports coaches sometimes come across as father figures – or big brothers?

The answer is yes – that is precisely the reason. Coaches will not just show you how to do things, but they will also push you to try your limit. They are still comfortable nosing around to understand your social life, and in that respect it does not actually pass as being nosy, as it is their business to know the characters you are associating with and the impact they are having on your mindset.

Sports coaches are famous. What else is coachable?

Oh –virtually everything! We have just mentioned how a coach helps you set the right working environment. So, if you are learning music, for example, and you pay for tuition classes, what you should expect is to learn the notes; the extent to which you open your mouth to release certain A-s and O-s; and that kind of thing.

But when you go out for a music coach, the guy is going to teach you the foods and drinks that you should spare your gullet; the kind of growling you should avoid no matter how upset someone makes you; how you should behave towards your colds; and such other things that are likely to have an impact on your voice box, your lungs, and all the other organs associated with release of sounds. Of course, this is not exclusive of the music skills. You will also be learning the necessary singing and instrumental skills.

Can you carry out coaching in the office?

Well, you can try... And you will succeed – if only you have got what it takes to wear two hats; one of the boss and another of the patron. Otherwise, do outsource the service.

We have mentioned sports and music already, and these two seem to be in a certain category that is different from matters of the office. You realize in the office is where you find the receptionists, secretaries, accountants, sales managers, operation managers, executive managers, and others, including an entire team of junior support staff. So, they are not a homogenous lot. The only point of convergence is that they work for you – or rather, they work for the organization that has made you boss.

Begin by knowing what you ultimately want to achieve

- You want your people to sharpen their skills and improve their abilities

- You want to help them sort out disturbing issues

- You want to show them how to go about tackling specific challenges

- You want to pre-empt any fall out amongst employees and between employees and the organization

- You want to improve the workers' overall performance

Can one or two coaches teach numbers of employees from different faculties effectively?

Well, they can. Coaches in the office do not teach accountants how to balance ledger books, and they do not aim to teach secretaries how to use letter heads – no. Rather, they have a way of beginning a sort of informal conversation between them and the employees, where they get to appreciate the prevailing challenges. In knowing those challenges, they then make suggestions on how those issues could be tackled. In the process, the individuals or groups come up with different scenarios and possible outcomes.

Ultimately, it is the employees themselves that make their pick. So, for a coach in the office, the responsibility is to help employees get into the mode of critical thinking – where they feel obliged to look for solutions; helping them take full charge of their role.

Chapter 2:
Laying the Ground for Coaching

Do you want to be a great coach? One thing you need to appreciate is that the only way you are going to make headway in any field is if the environment is conducive. Otherwise you will be running against a strong wind that counters most, if not all, of your efforts. That is not to undermine your competence and all, but really, whatever you have in your package will only benefit the person you are coaching if they are receptive.

Then again, you need to appreciate that for coaching to go well, both the coach and the person being coached need to be ready for it. And for sure, what strides can the coach make if the person being coached has no idea what coaching is all about?

Here is what everyone involved needs to know from the onset:

Be clear about what to expect from the coach

Coaching is not an ultimatum

Within the working environment, you need to make the employees understand that the coach is meant to help them deliver on their goals better and not to train them on how to do their job. If an employee is set to take on a new position, the understanding would be that the coach will prepare that employee to handle fresh responsibilities, which may be somewhat different from what they have always dealt with.

If the air is not cleared from the onset, the employees may have the perception that the coach has been sent to them to gather information and then provide feedback to management.

And most likely, they will suspect that such information is to be used to assess those the organization needs to lay off.

Of course, with that mindset, the employees being coached are unlikely to be sincere and open. In fact, they may even hold back some information, including challenges that they face in performing their duties. So, bluntly speaking, the coach is neither an inspector nor a witch hunter, and you need to make that crystal clear from the beginning.

Coaching is provided as a continuing support service

It is important that coaching be seen as a tool to help employees in their skill development and career in general. That means it is not helpful to have coaching being initiated just when everyone has condemned the section as failing. The minute management brings in a coach and the employees get the feeling the move is another way of saying shape up or you are out of here, not much progress will be forthcoming.

Of course, what may have triggered the need for a coach could be poor performance, but effort needs to be made to ensure the people being coached do not view the move as being either punitive or a threat.

Coaching is not meant to pre-empt legal action

If something needed to be done by management and was not done at the appropriate time, it is not reasonable that coaching should be used to camouflage the failure. If that is seen to be the case, or if the perception is that coaching is being provided to pre-empt legal action of sorts, the resources being used in this process will just be wasted; the coaching will not be helpful to either party.

Coaching needs to be supportive rather than remedial

Once you make coaching something that you do primarily to salvage a desperate situation, you will find yourself handling matters when crucial relationships have already suffered. As such, the coaching may not be very helpful. As a matter of practice, it is best to carry out coaching at the earliest convenient.

Employ a coach on the basis of relevance

What is the coach's expertise?

Do you find a retired professional basketball player coaching athletics? Surely no – it would raise eyebrows; and justifiably so. In the same vein, it does not seem logical that you should hire a sales person to coach an employee looking to take on a managerial position. You need a coach with the relevant expertise plus reasonable experience. And while trying to establish the coach's suitability, making a few calls to references is part of the bargain.

Is the coach's style suitable?

Please do not go looking for a suitable style because there cannot be a single one. It all depends on the person being coached. If, for instance, you are coaching people who have been delivering results on the basis of experience, having a young coach with big ideas on the science behind performance may not create a great relationship. On the contrary, you need a coach, young or old, who has the art of handling people in an open-minded manner.

In short, the coach needs to be flexible enough to be able to earn the trust of the people being coached. The coach's style should enable a relationship of mutual respect as well as trust.

Be on the same page with the coach

Do not send a coach blindly – lay out the context

A coach will be helpful to the person being coached and to the organization as well if only full disclosure is made on the reason the coaching is necessary. For example, someone being coached in preparation for a higher position needs a different approach from one who is being coached in order to raise productivity. It also needs to be different from a person being coached in preparation for a transfer to an area with a different culture.

Disclose pertinent issues

If, for example, the department has been experiencing internal conflict, it is best to let the coach be aware. It may sometimes even be a situation of an expanding workforce where the old personnel seem to be overshadowed. That information is important because therein might lie issues of mistrust. And with that inside information, the coach will be able to tailor his or her approach to suit the situation.

Disclose any improvement steps taken

If the coaching is meant to straighten some rough patches, the coach needs to be aware of any other steps that have been taken before; including the specific period they took place. Even the administrative steps fall into this scope. However, it is important to appreciate that just because coaching is taking place does not relieve the supervisors or managers of their supervisory roles.

How do the employee and immediate supervisor get along?

The coach needs to know the kind of relationship that exists between the individual employees and their supervisors. If it is strained the coach will, definitely, tailor the coaching in a way that will address the situation. Likewise, if it is too close the coach will make a point of addressing it too so that the employee can take the supervisor's role with the seriousness it deserves.

How much does the employee know about the coaching?

It is imperative that you let the coach know what the employee has been told about the coaching. When you know the employee's perspective and expectations, then the journey to success is set as you will be working along the same lines.

Get the employee ready

Inform the employee of the coaching in advance

It is advisable that you let your employee know there is a coach set to call on them and work with them. And it is at that juncture that you explain why the coaching sessions are deemed necessary. Let the employee also feel that their voice can be heard regarding the timing as well as the venue.

The point here is that you need to avoid a scenario where the employee feels hijacked or even like a victim of a conspiracy. And that is precisely what would happen if the first time the employee hears about the coaching is in the presence of the coach; probably when the sessions are beginning.

Do not make a coaching session an additional meeting

You need to let your employee know the specific expectations for the coaching. For instance, spell out, in case the coaching is at the proposal stage, that you expect fast response about how interested the employee is. Also make it known that you expect the employee to adhere to agreed schedules without unnecessary lateness and cancellations. It is also important that the employee participates actively by asking questions and being receptive to feedback.

What is the coaching set to achieve?

It is important to have clear goals

Once goals are clear, both the coach and the employee can tell when they have made headway. Management too can tell.

Let the goals be the same for all parties

Having management set goals that are different from those of the employee cannot be good for the organization. This issue needs to be discussed. If, for instance, it is a case of the employee preparing to take up a new role, it is important that his or her expectations be those of the management; and where they differ, they need to discuss and find common ground.

Coach should identify needs

Usually a coach helps to streamline issues of employee behavior in the prevailing circumstances. However, in the process of coaching, certain issues may be revealed that only management can address. For instance, you may have a wonderful employee who, despite being devoted to the company, feels disadvantaged by the organization's remuneration structure. That is something that the coach may advice management upon.

The coach needs the ear of senior management

For coaching to yield the desired results, any deep seated issues the employee has and which may inhibit the proper progress of the coaching need to be reported to senior management; that is, above the employee's immediate supervisor or manager. Discussing such details with the immediate supervisor or manager would be tantamount to breaching confidentiality and that would even make the employee lose trust in the coach.

Coaching is not magic

Coaching is not like instant coffee that produces a beverage instantly. With coaching, all parties need to be aware that results can only show after a while. And so management should not begin getting anxious of not seeing instant change from the employees involved. Rather, it is important that they be patient and they also render all the support possible so that the coached employees can find a supportive environment to implement what they learnt from the coaching.

How far should confidentiality go?

Coach needs to keep the employees information confidential

It needs to be spelt out from the beginning that all matters the employee discloses in conversation with the coach are to be treated as confidential by the coach. That makes the employee free to open up and volunteer information that can prove useful to the coaching process.

The employee is not restricted by confidentiality

As for the employee, there is freedom to share whatever is discussed or learnt from the coaching sessions with any person they choose, including top management. On the other hand, they are not obligated to discuss it either.

Feedback to supervisors or managers need to be general

Even as feedback is expected after every assignment, from the coach to the seniors of the employee, it should be presented in general terms. For instance, it needs to be in terms of whether the employee adhered to schedules; was an active participant; was receptive; and so on. The details of what transpired are not to be disclosed.

There needs to be an exception clause for confidentiality

There are cases where the coach may feel the necessity to disclose information gained in the course of coaching, like if there is a risk of someone getting injured or in there is concealed ongoing abuse in the workplace. To cater for such circumstances, the coach needs to be officially protected in his or her terms of engagement.

Spell out when the coach can terminate the contract prematurely

The situations where the coach is mandated to disclose acquired information, is mentioned earlier, is when the client is at risk of harm or other people are. How about if the client is involved in behavior that happens to be unacceptable in the coach's opinion? Confidentiality must still be maintained. However, the coach could encourage the employee to do the disclosing personally otherwise the coach brings the sessions to a halt. The coach can actually give the employee an ultimatum for this.

The coaching goals should suit all group members

Although coaching is not an information dissemination program, you need to have people with a common purpose just like a class. The group members may, for instance, belong to the same department; be a group of people set to take up managerial positions soon; be people set to work on a common project; and so on.

In group coaching, the coach needs to focus primarily on what affects the group and not the individual. If the individual's behavior or approach is to be addressed, it should be only as far as it has an impact on the success of the group.

It needs to be mentioned, however, that the individuals in the group need to be guided on how to make the best use of their talents and skills because in the process the overall group benefits; and the group fulfills its goals more efficiently.

A coach is set to succeed despite changing circumstances

A coach needs to be prepared for challenges

A good coach is not expected to take a template with him or her for the employees to complete. It is the coach to adjust to the client's environment and help out within the prevailing circumstances. So, if a coach finds an unexpected situation, it is up to him or her to adjust accordingly.

A coach needs to exercise patience

Whereas the guidance of a coach can begin to produce positive results within a short time, the real impact is usually felt long after the coaching sessions are done. That is something that the employee concerned, the management and the coach need to understand.

Chapter 3: What Is the Importance of Coaching?

Oh, how many times have you woken up feeling like you would not, if only you had a choice? So you go to the office only because you are not ready to lose your job, or you attend a sports training session only because you do not want to risk being chucked from the team when you miss the training. So, many are the times you keep to the straight path only because you have an overseer. But would you not enjoy a situation where you were excited to jump out of bed and get on with business? This is one of the things that a coach tries to do: get you to a place where you feel motivated to work or do whatever it is you have chosen to do.

And if you love something, why would you need someone else to push you?

No – a coach does not really push you; at least not in the sense of forcing. The thing is – there are some challenges that come your way even when you did not sign for them. Consider this:

You are trying to do your best in school basketball with the hope of being identified for NBA. Yet apart from one or two of your friends, and of course, your ever loyal mum, everyone else can only enumerate how many 6-footers never made it beyond college basketball, and how marginal your chances are of joining any top team. That is called discouragement and negative vibe.

- Hopes are what they are. And so, for example, if you are hoping to join the NBA some day, you still cannot afford to slacken on your studies, for you know not if this basketball dream will come true. What would happen if you never got to join the league? You, definitely, would need to have professional papers to make it in life.

Now this is where pressure comes in. No parent sends their kid to school to play basketball, soccer or whatever else. They send them to do academics; and the rest is just but incidental. And the pressure to maintain good academic grades and keep up your sport practice can be overwhelming.

- Just because you have joined a sports team does not uproot you from the society. So things that are happening in the community around you get to you and have an impact on your mood, your attitude, and even your level of motivation. If, for instance, you have a brother who is vying for a political seat, and then either on TV or on social media you see reports of how someone had thrown rotten eggs his way, it would definitely get you off focus. And right there I can almost hear your breathing as you expend masses of negative energy.

The coach's role:

When such distractions occur, your coach helps you to downplay them. Not assuming they do not exist – no; just ensuring that you deal with them in a way that does not adversely affect your chosen pursuit.

- A coach helps you to direct your thoughts to the goal that matters most at the time; keeping you least distracted.

- A coach helps you to channel your energy to your chosen cause. For example, if you keep paying attention to opposing fans and responding to them, you will not have enough energy to improve your act.

- A coach helps you to remain focused. If you have a politician brother, for example, the coach makes you appreciate the need to chart your own success path as opposed to being absorbed in your brother's fame. You get to hear the hard reality that even if you were to twist your leg on the court, your politician brother would not resign from Congress, Senate or whatever other office he may be holding. Likewise, you should not miss your training session just because the politicians are playing dirty in their arena.

In short, you get to learn that there are some negatives that come with every territory, and that it is fine to let those in the kitchen deal with the heat while you do what you have got to do. In summary, this is what you discuss and agree on with your coach:

- What do you really want to achieve?

- What obstacles are you encountering or envisaging?

- What action do you need to take to decimate those obstacles and pave way for your success?

In general, coaching is about making inquiries into your perception, abilities, commitment and challenges, and leading you to reflecting on the whole situation. And in interrogating the situation of the person you are coaching, you need to frame your questions in certain ways in order to be able to receive answers that are relevant and useful.

We shall, therefore, discuss different kinds of questions because sometimes you want to get the person opening up in an unrestricted manner, and other times you want to, more or less, direct the person's line of thought. Of course you appreciate that a question is not simply a question. There are those that you throw in the air just to keep the conversation going. Think of the rhetorical questions, for example: *How could you have retained him as manager anyway?* Here, you are not expecting your trainee to give you any answers because what you imply with that question is that nobody would have expected you to retain the person in question as your manager.

On the contrary, there are those questions that are geared towards extracting information from the person you are coaching. How you frame such questions matters; and how you follow up their answers also matters. And that is why it is very important that you pay keen attention to your trainee's verbal answer and body language too.

Chapter 4:
How Curious Questions Help in Coaching

John, why did you pull the tail while your teammates seemed to run with so much ease?

If someone were to ask you that in the name of being a coach, I doubt that you would return for another coaching session much as you are dying to win races. In the meantime, the coach is waiting for your answer, so you must say something. And your answer, as a sensitive human being, is likely to lean on the defensive. The whole question sounds accusatory. In fact most questions that begin with the word *why* straight away trigger some defensive reaction.

Still, we need to appreciate that curious questions must be skewed towards digging out answers from the person being coached. As such, the questions begin with:

- What?

- How?

- When?

- Why?

- Supposing...?

What other qualities befit a good curious question? Well, they need to be:

- Short – with a length of, say, ten words or even fewer.

- Concise – well, carrying full message or impact, though short.

- Carrying a clear message; hitting the nail on the head.

- Open-ended: meaning that you leave room for the other person to volunteer information – the kind of question whose answers can emerge from different perspectives. Just to make it clear, curious questions should not be satisfied by a mere *yes* or *no*.

- And why does a coach need to use open-ended questions here? Well – the reason is that the aim of curious questions is to jog your mind into looking at issues in a fresh perspective; possibly an angle you have not considered before.

Alright! We now know what curious questions are and what their importance is. But you know what? We still have a problem of putting people on their defensive by asking them *why*. How do we circumvent that problem so that we can get objective answers?

Easy – just being a little creative with speech. Get yourself to play ignorant – which you really are in regard to this person – and inquire about plausible causes. For example:

What reasons would you attribute to ...

Wow! This kind of question comes across as an innocent inquiry; yet it answers the *why* you wanted without you coming across as passing judgment.

Sample Curious Questions

- What race do you want to run this season?

- What medal are you aiming for?

- What challenges did you face last season?

- When do you plan on starting training?

- What reasons do you have for preferring that time?

- How do you determine the best training ground?

- Suppose you considered varying your training hours.

- Have you ever considered changing careers?

- How do you think your life would change if you got married?

- What are you prepared to sacrifice to get to the top?

- What have you been thinking since your last defeat?

- How would you feel if you made the cut for CEO?

- Is there another career you think you could fit in?

- Why do you think they have kept you on despite the challenges?

- How do you think they are going to conduct the process?

These sample questions seem to fit the bill. Yet, there is something else you cannot ignore. The core reason you are coaching is that you want to motivate someone. Now if you dish out a flurry of mundane questions, the guy is likely to gape at you and start wondering what difference there is between you and the patrol police. So:

- Can you try and be somewhat creative in the way you design your questions.

- You also need to capitalize on the answers you receive, picking a word or two from there to base your subsequent questions on. That way, you sort of create a conversation rather than making the whole session sound like an interrogation.

- You need to restrict yourself to one question at a time.

- You need to keep your questions simple. By all means, fight the temptation to ask a question and explaining it and sort of suggesting answers, and so on. If you do that, the questions may sound boring, sometimes leading (lawyers' language), and at worst, simply winding and confusing.

Above everything we have said, do your best to be empathetic. That is the main factor that will get you places. If you are talking to me and I detect empathy, I am likely to open up to you. You may even be surprised to hear me talk non-stop like a parrot.

Wow! Great news there – for every coach wants you answering questions freely and openly. The challenge now is for you to practice the art of empathetic listening.

What is empathetic listening anyway?

Well, it is simply active listening; listening that is reflective. Plainly speaking, it is the kind of listening that shows the speaker that the message is sinking and not just flapping on your outer ear and going off with the wind. It is only when you listen empathetically that you give answers and comments that are apt and relevant. And believe you me, everyone can tell when you are listening empathetically as opposed to when you are struggling to keep mum, eager to say your next piece.

What is the impact of empathetic listening?

- It helps to build trust between you and the person you are coaching.

- It actually releases any tension that may have built up between the two of you.

- It helps the other person to relax and openly portray genuine emotions.

- It gets the other person opening up so freely, sometimes letting information flow out like water through an open valve. This is the time when the person's attitudes, fears, biases and probably prejudices reflect clearly like sunrays against a mirror.

- It creates an environment conducive for objective discussion, which makes it easy for the two of you to solve problematic issues in a mutual way. And this is the basis of effective coaching.

How, then do you get to practice genuine empathetic listening?

Great question – for what is the use of holding an air ticket if you cannot make your way to the airport? For someone to feel that sincere empathy, it is imperative that you:

- Respond using words that indicate you have grasped what the person just said. You could even mention some words or phrases that the person just used.

- Let your body language adjust with the emotions of the person's message, even as you encourage the speaker to go on telling more.

- Avoid interrupting the person when he or she is in the element. Information is hard to come by and so you better allow free speech when the opportunity has availed itself.

- Try to fit into the shoes of your subject in order to appreciate the person's point of view.

The long and short of this empathy thing is to let the person you are set to coach know that you are eager to hear what he or she is saying, and that you are not going to play judge. Even then, you should not misconstrue that to mean that you are ready to concur with all details given and to adopt all attitudes portrayed. Far from that – yours is to express in word, body language and deed, your willingness to be a resource person for your learner.

Chapter 5:
How Clarifying Questions Help the Coaching Process

What are they, these clarifying questions? It sounds like you have actually heard something from your subject, but you cannot repeat the message with confidence because some things have not come out clearly. And that is alright because, really, coaching needs to be carried out like a normal conversation. And this is where clarifying questions come in.

The trick – well, not trick but wisdom; or maybe it really is a trick – well, the whole intent is to have your guy delve deeper into the subject, bringing out that which he or she may have been hesitant to disclose. For instance, you may have begun to coach a lady who has just changed managers. When she says something like *my relationship with my manager became strained*, it would be a good idea to follow it up with a clarifying – in fact, probing – question.

You realize there are a hundred and one possibilities why such a relationship could become strained beginning with the manager's failing loyalty, drunkenness, misappropriation of funds and so on. So you may wish to frame your question thus: *What would you say caused the strain between you and your manager?*

And you may get an eye opening response that makes you understand your learner's circumstances even better. She might, for example, clarify to you that her manager had actually become her husband, the two having developed a romantic relationship in the course of the professional one; and he had probably turned controlling and dictatorial. There may even be issues of infidelity involved, which, in such circumstances inevitably cause negative emotions to spill over into the professional arena.

In a different scenario where you may be coaching an entrepreneur, you could ask about the source of the venture capital; and your trainee may tell you that it was provided by the parents. Here, you may wish to pose a clarifying question: *Am I to understand that the money from your parents was free?*

And you could find yourself receiving a very enlightening response like:

Actually, it was a loan that I had promised to repay in three years.

Or

Yes, it was free; but it was on condition that I finance their annual holiday abroad for the remaining part of their life.

Of course how you approach the discussion on someone who is heavily indebted and one who is free of debt is bound to be different. Likewise, the way you tailor your coaching when someone has an important obligation to someone else is different from one who has no dependant or obligation.

Here are some sample clarifying questions:

- Did you actually say that...?

- Am I to understand that the amount you owe...?

- Would I be correct then to say that...?

- What was the exact amount of damages awarded by the court?

- Have you ever tried an alternative method?

- Is it true to say that you have now severed links with...?

- Who else do you plan to bring on board?

- Would you mind if someone gave you a different opinion?

- Is that your wish or something you have actually tried before?

- Who else in the group do you think sabotages your efforts?

- Is it really sabotage or your perceived ineptitude that made them overlook you for promotion?

- Would you really like to compete against them or you are just trying to be polite?

- Is beige your color or you took that for lack of a choice?

- Did they actually express displeasure or did you deduce from their facial expressions?

- Would they be justified, then, to relieve you of your duties?

Sometimes you are not just seeking clarification but actually trying to interrogate the circumstances further. This is the time you use questions that are outright probing such as:

- What criteria did you apply in choosing a manager?

- Why do you think you have been on a losing streak this season?

- How do you think changing your training ground would impact your performance?

- Why do you think they want you to be the team captain?

- How did it happen that your grievances reached the federation?

- How did you come to the conclusion that ...?

- At the time of the incident, what was the relationship between ...?

- What would you do if this method did not bear fruit?

As you may have already noticed, there is no single question here that can be satisfied with a single word or two. Each of them actually calls for analytical thinking before answering. They, therefore, pave the way for undisclosed information to come out.

That is where you get to learn, for instance, that the entrepreneur who has sought your expertise because his business is going down despite massive investment has actually been out of circulation, having been incarcerated for six months. In short, you get to learn that what he is telling you about the business is what he has been fed with by those who were running the business in his absence. And, granted, that could be credible or not. At this juncture then, you realize you have got to get the true picture in other ways, to be able to help this guy.

Chapter 6:
How Do Possibility Questions Help?

Do you like it when you get a lot of information from the person you are trying to coach? What a question! This is one of those rhetorical ones, isn't it? Of course you are pleased to gather as much information as you can because it enhances your understanding of the person you are dealing with, both professionally and socially. Now, if you have noticed the nature of the questions that bring out such vast information, you will realize they are open-ended. This means that, as the person being coached, you can touch on all and sundry in your response.

Whereas that is helpful to your coach, it is not good that it continues uncontrolled. If it does, you will be telling stories with your coach all day long, giving opinions and ideas from a whole range of perspectives. Therefore, the questions need to be streamlined as you seek to come up with deductions; because obviously, the reason you sign in for coaching is to get solutions to problems – ways of streamlining your activities thus leading to your success. Deductions, or the conclusions you come up with between you and your coach, are instrumental in setting the way forward.

Just compare these two questions:

a) When do you think we should begin?

b) Do you think we should begin by 20th – or is that too late?

When you ask the kind of questions as in (a) above, you should be ready to get dates within any imaginable range. For example, it may be January now, but the person could suggest to you a date around end of the month or even end of the year; and both dates are justifiable considering the way you framed your question.

But in (b) above, you have already suggested a date range. So, your listener will consider the dates with a view to either accepting the 20th of January, or bringing his or her suggestion much closer than that. Such are the questions we refer to as possibility questions. Can you see that in (b) we are already visualizing the possibility of 20th being too far? And with such a suggestion, you are guiding your trainee on the best time frame without dictating it.

If we have not mentioned it before, you need to realize that your trainee is likely to adhere to timeframes that he or she has suggested than if the dates were simply provided for adherence. So what you do is frame your questions right, where *right* here means guiding your trainee's thinking.

Plainly speaking, this is what you should expect from open-ended questions:

- A personal response reflecting biases, prejudices, emotions and so on.

- An answer whose length you cannot determine in advance – could be a short story or a brief paragraph.

- Genuine, sincere, original, unguarded answers.

- Answers that you possibly least expected.

It looks that we could summarize this by saying that with open-ended questions you should expect virtually anything.

On the contrary, this is what you should expect possibility questions to provoke:

- Answers that are well targeted; portraying a sense of conclusion.

- Answers with limited dialogue, which is narrowed towards a particular clear direction.

- Answers that suggest some action or way forward.

The idea, generally, is for you to have the open-ended questions earlier on in your conversation, and then towards the end, you shoot your possibility questions. Remember, as a coach, you are doing all this in a relatively relaxed environment. So you have all along avoided the kind of questionnaire banks send to their clients – very specific, as in either this or nothing; or the kind of questioning that auditors pose to their subjects – sometimes injuriously probing. It is safe to say that the coaching atmosphere is friendly.

Again, we have said plenty here that brings out the fact that when you are a coach you surely are no doctor – do not prescribe. If you do, it must be in a snaky way – yeah: slithering your way around until you get your trainee to see what is best for them. Anyway, since that analogy may remind you of vile deeds of that reptile, let us just say you use your wit to lead your trainee and have him or her come up with suggestions that you personally think are best for them. And the way you do it is by tapping into the information you have already gotten out of them, and then designing your possibility question suggestively. Of course you do not tell them I would rather you did this and I'm wondering if you concur – no!

- You ask a question and provide a suggestion

- You ask a question with alternative answers

See some sample Possibility Questions below:

- Do you wish to sign the contract now or would you rather you consulted your parents first?

- Do you prefer to invite them this month or that particular month or that other particular month?

- Are you going to give a press statement this week or would you rather you waited to see the direction the media debate takes?

- Does the resignation of so-and-so bother you or do you like the opportunity to engage someone younger?

- Does the leakage of that story disturb you or are you going to ride on it to gain popularity?

- If you were to choose between the branches to work in, would you choose one in Latin America, one in Africa or one in India?

- On a scale of 1 – 5 how do you rate the current officials?

- Is this course something you love or are you taking it to get far away from home?

- Are you optimistic about this season with your new tutor or do you think the sudden change is likely to adversely affect your performance?

- Is this your sincere belief or are you taking the stand to cool their tempers?

- If the rugby team offered to take you now that you are playing football, would you switch to rugby or you would remain loyal to the game that has made you this successful?

- Will the expedition to the Alps benefit you or are you going to take your trainer with you?

There is an infinite number of possibility questions you could ask, but you confine yourself to those that suit your situation. And since what you are interested in is to finally help your client, do not feel gagged or restricted in modifying your questions. Different people could be aroused differently by the same questions depending on a number of things, including the state of mind of each one of them.

Therefore, feel free to add some flesh to your question even after you have said it. If the question was one with options, you could always add another option or two into the mix, as long as it is geared towards helping your client make a beneficial choice.

Chapter 7:
Qualities of a Good Coach

Who is a good coach? You can simply say that a good coach is one who is able to make his or her clients succeed. The question is what is it that the coach does to make the client successful? Besides knowing how to frame questions in order to extract much needed information from the client, what else is required?

First of all, it is good to be practical and acknowledge that most organizations do not have a budget for external coaching. Many are those that leave the coaching to respective department managers who are assumed to have something helpful to impart to their juniors. The problem here is that coaching is not necessarily mentoring. And as already mentioned it is not tutoring either. It is, therefore, important that those managers bestowed upon the role of coaching know clearly what is expected of them in this regard.

An Executive Coaching Survey done in 2010 indicated that 63% of significant organizations rely on internal coaching. And even amongst those ones, about half of them invest barely 10% or less of their time in coaching. Maybe coaching could be taken more seriously if it was clear what it aims to achieve.

How coaching helps:

It raises the employee's level of effectiveness at work

If every employee were to be effective, would that not define the organization's success? After all, the success of an entity is the sum total of the success of all departments under which employees work.

It gets the employee to think more broadly

This means that the employee will be able to link his or her input to the organization's overall success. This is different from when an employee sees his or her duties as isolated chores to be accomplished day by day or month by month. Again, it is in this broad way of thinking that an employee learns to improvise when certain resources are not available and adjust when things do not run as preset.

It recognizes an employee's strengths

How many employees are paid but underutilized just because of some organizational protocol or just because nobody realizes what a resource the person is? Such talent can be identified for more appropriate roles. While making the employee more comfortable, such a move would also be geared towards benefiting the organization more.

Coaching brings out any need there is for development

There are times you have a good employee who would be invaluable to the company if only they were better trained or better orientated. Whatever is the case, it can be discovered during coaching.

Setting challenging targets

Coaching is a two way experience and both the manager in charge of coaching and the employee being coached can settle on target goals during the coaching process. This would be fine because they have room to discuss what the hindrance would be and how to tackle them; and also what resources would be required to make them attain their goal.

At the end of the coaching process, the coach should be satisfied that he or she is leaving behind a person who is growing. The fact that the employee can think critically and be ready to make decisions that they can stand by is indication of successful coaching.

Research from the Center for Creative Leadership has summed up the skills managers need in order to play marvelous coaches; and they are:

Managing to earn much needed trust as well as respect from employees

To have the employees trust you, it is imperative that you set your boundaries as their senior and also to keep your promises. You surely cannot be the guy who staggers home in drunkenness from the same pub your employees frequent and expect to maintain respectable boundaries.

What happens when they have to drag you to your car all lost and unruly? And what happens when you promise study leave that you have not even agreed with top management and then it does not get authorized? In short, for your employees to benefit from your coaching endeavors, you need to build a relationship of mutual respect and trust.

Ability to make measurable assessment

The manager should be able to provide objective feedback on what the employee is missing out to reach the required level of performance, and then discuss with the employee possible steps to be taken to amend that. After a reasonable duration, the manager should be able to make another assessment so that the employee can know how his or her efforts have impacted performance. In short, the following questions should acquire answers within reasonable timelines:

- What were you unable to achieve as an employee and you are now achieving it?

- What did you promise to do and you actually implemented it?

- What were your intentions and were they realized?

Ability to get employees thinking critically

Here what is meant is particularly the skill to ask open ended questions. That means the employee has room to go beyond a yes or a no in response. The employee can engage his or her mind and give sincere observation and deductions. On encouraging this kind of thinking, the coach also encourages decision making based on reasonable assessment of a situation – and that includes a level of risk taking.

Being supportive

The coaching manager is expected to be open minded as they listen to their employees, and be able to empathize with them. The trust they have earned should be enough to encourage the employees to ventilate without fearing that they will be judged adversely. Without a doubt, it is easier to assist someone make progress when you know what their frustrations are than otherwise. And in this spirit of being supportive, the manage needs to acknowledge good work and achievement of goals.

Helping to achieving goals

It is not enough for a manager to point fingers to a failing workforce. As a coaching manager, when your employees achieve their goals, it is your success too. And the reverse is applicable. For that reason, one measure of your great coaching skills is your underlings' success in meeting set targets.

Chapter 8:
Common Coaching Challenges and How to Handle Them

Do you think coaching is something every employee will embrace? If you think about the many unvoiced complaints that employees have from feeling under-remunerated to being in the wrong job, you will see why they would shun any additional engagement, without giving it a chance. How about where individuals voluntarily hire coaches – are there challenges? Definitely, there are challenges because some people only hear that having a coach leads to success. However, they fail to understand that a coach is not a magician and cannot work alone. So there are myriad reasons that make a coach's job one big challenge.

Here are some:

Client not being committed

How can you get an athlete, for instance, to reduce his or her personal best time by, say, a minute or two, if they are not willing to maintain a regular rest schedule?

Client having a procrastinating tendency

If you agree that the client is to begin training at a certain date and then that changes without good notice, and not once or twice, that is an ominous sign for a coach. It means the coach is dealing with an unpredictable client. How can the coach even be sure of consistency once the coaching begins? Often, it may just be a sign of the client developing cold feet not knowing what to expect.

Inability to communicate effectively

A client who cannot speak out sincerely and without fear makes it difficult for the coach to decipher the weaknesses that need to be addressed. It follows then that improvement takes time and the client in turn begins to feel exasperated. Now, with both coach and the client feeling frustrated, what success can this coaching engagement produce?

A client having no clue about coaching

When someone identifies natural talent and remarks that if you had a coach you would do marvelous, this is not enough for you to be the best unless you first all charter a way forward. You need to know where you stand amongst other competitors, what you have achieved so far and where you need to be within a certain period. And this is what you need to let your coach know. With that knowledge then, you can have an idea the point at which you are starting and the point you would like to reach. With specific direction, the coach will find it easy to assist.

Some clients are not proactive

As mentioned before, there are some clients who think that coaches come with an instant solution. It then becomes a big challenge to get the client do his or her part with that kind of mentality. Nobody ever got to make them understand that no success comes without effort.

However, as long as the coach can anticipate challenges of this nature, they will be able to think ahead of ways to counter them and get the client succeeding despite a bumpy beginning.

43

Here are ways out for coaches:

As a coach, lay out a vivid picture of the final outcome

Once the client can see the enviable image of success, they are likely to push excuses aside and focus on attaining the goal. It is actually a great way of motivating the client though it looks more like bait.

Have tiny goals first

It is understandable that one should be scared of how high a target is, especially if it is nothing close to where they are at the moment. The solution, however, is to break down the long term goal into small goals that are achievable within a relatively short time. As a coach you should be able to spell out the achievements to look out for after such a short spell. The gratifying news, however, is that success, irrespective of how tiny it may appear, is motivating to the performer. In any case, succeeding in many successive tiny steps is the sure way of accomplishing the bigger goal.

Apply your communication techniques

The coach needs to apply all the communication techniques he knows to get the client to open up. This is where the personality of the coach comes in because a good one will be able even to alter his style to suit the personality of the particular client. He could, for instance:

- Request for client's feedback at regular intervals

- Adopt the communication style where you keep paraphrasing what you deem as what your client means, and of course ask the client to confirm that.

- Volunteer exciting ideas and see if any of them stimulates your client into communicating more

- Keep giving opinions and insights to try and provoke your client into participating

- Inquire into vocational skills that your client has

- Inquire into what makes your client tick

At the end of the day, you will be able, as a coach, to assist your client come up with a Purpose Statement, so that both of you know where you stand and where you are headed.

Chapter 9:
How a Coach Can Improve Your Cash Flow

You really are thinking of hiring a coach to show you how to make money? That is something that can send skeptics chuckling. They might think it is sheer waste of money, or probably something just elitist. But little do they know that they may end up going in circles while you use the coach's guidance to improve your earnings; recoup the resources you spent on the coach; and have your business flourishing in record time.

When it comes to success in business, if you get an opportunity, you could get great guidance from successful business people who will point out what they tried and got burnt and where they touched and money began flooding in. Again, with today's open communication channels you can enlist the services of a business coach from any part of the world irrespective of where you reside. The question is will you be paying for quality coaching or for a quack in the field?

Here is what you need to assess before settling on a business coach:

What can the person show as proof of professional competence?

Granted it may not be always that you demand to see a professional certificate, but can you please verify in a credible manner that the guy is coaching someone else and that you are not paying to be his or her guinea pig? Establish too if he is known to give lectures in the relevant field.

And while doing your due diligence, do analyze the services attributed to this person. If they touch on this, that and that other thing in this, that and that other field, that should be a red flag right there. You are not looking for a jack of all trades for a coach, or, are you?

Assess the person's readiness to share

Wherever you plan on getting your coach, have a discussion and assess how much they are willing to disclose about their life or their involvement in business. Anyone who just wants you to swallow what they tell you and seeming to be unsettled by questions is not a good choice. A good coach is pretty transparent and comfortable with questions.

Establish the person is experienced

You cannot purport to lead someone along a road you have not personally traveled and so it is important that the person you intend to hire as a coach shows you proof of having been tried. References also come in handy. And nothing would be as comforting as hearing testimony from someone who has been led by that coach and succeeded. And nothing would beat a warning from someone who has been messed up by a pseudo coach.

Get someone with a good attitude

Much as you are ready to toe the line and be respectful to your coach, you do not, on the other hand, want to have someone who makes you feel like you are walking on eggshells. If the guy cannot stomach a bit of humor or even cynicism, he is not the right choice. You need to commit to working with someone that can stomach your attitude when you feel discouraged and pessimistic, and someone who will still persist on bringing you back on board no matter how rough the road proves to be. That is why you may need to let the greenhorns pass as they may still have some reality to learn above having professional papers.

Check out a coach with some good network

Look – opening income streams is usually a matter of opportunities. And while you can succeed with a wild card every now and then, when it comes to business, it is often a matter of whom you know and whom you can trust. So having a coach who knows some people who matter in the business arena could get you fruitful connections. Sometimes just one link to the right people may get your business soaring in ways you never dreamt of.

Establish accessibility

You surely cannot afford to engage a coach who will be available to you in a very limited way. So you need to discuss that upfront to establish you are not talking of a guy who is overcommitted in terms of clients or someone who has other tight personal commitments. And if that happens to be the case, you may need to rethink. Being able to reach your coach conveniently is important because a word from him or her could mean you committing yourself to a contract or turning it down; and in business, as usual, time is of essence.

Know what the coach expects of you

If while doing your assessment you realize the person has no demands to make on you as the person to be coached, be wary. How then is he or she going to measure your progress?

Assess the coach's commitment

One of the ways to know if your coach is committed to his or her job is observing how he keeps his or her appointments with you. Another thing is the person's demeanor. Someone who displays impatience and inability to express themselves as well as a good teacher should is questionable. If you can register that in the early stages, what is bound to happen once the contract is on? You are better off playing safe.

Chapter 10:
How to Identify a Good Health Coach

Health is nothing to joke around with. Of course, often people tend to think about the money, but your health is directly about your life. Hence, it calls for more care in selecting your health coach than any other coach. Or do you want to hire someone to help you keep fit and then you end up losing carefully built muscle and becoming unhealthy instead?

The kind of person you are seeking as your health coach is not someone who is in it just for the money. Rather, it should be someone who:

Values everything to do with health

Do you find your gym instructor so amiable and dedicated that you imagine he or she could make a great health coach? Well, efficiency at the gym is not sufficient to give you the proper picture. A good health coach needs to be conversant with the calls made by the dietician and also with your state of mind. In short, even as exercising is a great part of keeping healthy, there is more to it that your health coach should be able and willing to address. Having the complete package is what will get you optimum results that are also sustainable.

Is passionate

You want someone who is passionate about seeing you attain your goal; someone who is capable of motivating you. The fact is if it is just information you wanted you could bury yourself in a library. But what you need is someone with the inspiration and energy to get you to translate great information into action.

Is abreast with modern information and trends

Surely you cannot be comfortable with a graduate who does not refresh his or her knowledge as new research findings are released and new methods of doing things tested. You would rather have a coach who tells you, hold on a minute, I'll find out that one from the recent findings. Then you know you are dealing with a person dedicated to learning and gaining fresh information.

Is great at listening

If in your very first interaction the person displays an attitude of *I'm the expert let me talk*, that is a sign of trouble. You want someone who will listen to your concerns and help you in your unique situation and not lump you among all other clients. Why bother paying for a private health coach who has just one prescription for every client? A health coach is helpful when he or she is capable of listening to you with an open mind.

Here are tips you could use in getting a good health coach

Seek someone who has walked your path

You will, definitely, strike a chord with someone who has experienced the challenges you are facing and for which you need a coach. So when it comes to, say, cravings of a certain nature, they get you right away. Without that you may end up with a coach whom you can see clearly is struggling to be patient with you when you fall off the wagon. And the least you need when you are struggling with matters of health is a judgmental coach.

Check out someone with a free test run

Confident coaches often give you an opportunity to test their services. And even when that is online, you could get at least half an hour for free consultation. The interaction during that period should give you a pretty good idea if that is someone you could work with. Ask yourself:

- Does he or she seem to listen to me or is he or she just dishing out standard answers?

- Do I feel objectivity or does this coach come across as judgmental?

- Does she make you feel like speaking your heart out?

- Do her questions trigger deeper thinking on your part?

Of course, you want to work with someone you feel comfortable with; someone who makes you feel like pouring out your frustrations and hopes; someone not judgmental; and someone who gets you thinking analytically and critically about your life.

Check what credentials your potential coach has

At times you will find those on the person's website and other times you could check them out under various professional bodies. Of course, here you could also seek confirmation or otherwise from references. Discussing independently with some people who happen to have gone through the hands of this person can give you either an assurance or a warning.

Do some testing in different ways

How about subscribing to this person's newsletter? No doubt its content coupled with the way it is laid out can give you an idea what the person means by quality of content. It can also give you an idea the depth of relevant knowledge this person possesses. You could even become a participant on their business social media pages, say face book, twitter and so on. This virtual interaction will mirror the person reasonably.

Avoid the temptation to use pricing as your measure

Who wants to save a dollar here and another there? Makes good spending sense... However, in some areas like health, cheap offers can turn out to be, on the contrary, expensive. So it may be advisable to bring the issue of pricing down the list of factors you are weighing. In fact, a good coach whatever his or her price, is expected to leave you in a position where you can progress alone confidently.

That means he or she will have disseminated great information to you; showed you how to handle different tough situations; and also enhanced your personal confidence. So, it definitely is worth paying somewhat more to someone who leaves you grounded than less on someone who leaves you still dependent.

Chapter 11:
What You Need To Know About Spiritual Life Coaching

Did you have breakfast this morning? Have you completed reading a document you started the other day; or even an assignment that you had; and possibly mended a fence that happened to be falling? Great deeds they all are. However, is that everything you are meant to do? At some point you enjoy your meals but then sooner than later you go hungry yet again. You read some document this moment and yet there are many more you will not have read – so you do not feel fulfilled. You mend a fence today and in a couple of months it is fallen yet again. And it really does not matter whether the fence drops again after a couple of years – you will still feel like you are actually going through this life in a circular form. What, say then, would really make you fulfilled? Which thing or action is it that will give your life a deeper meaning? Simple: It is spirituality.

Spirituality – well, meaning Christianity? Maybe Hinduism...? But no – spirituality is not about religion or a ritualistic tradition. It is about looking upon a higher being for guidance, knowledge and protection. And once you believe in that higher being, what you may wish to call the Divine, you appreciate there is a life beyond the physical; beyond the material things that you work for and accumulate. At the same time, you appreciate there is an important reason you are here today, that is, in this physical world. And the reason you eat, drink and clothe yourself is to keep in shape to be able to fulfill that bigger mission. In short, without the bigger mission your life lacks serious meaning.

It is in that quest for your purpose that you feel the urge to explore the higher realms of existence, those that connect you to everyone else and to everything in the universe. That is a humbling experience but one that fills the vacuum that would otherwise exist within you. And this is the stage at which the question comes what spiritual life coaching is all about.

Of what significance is a spiritual life coach?

To help you identify your purpose

A spiritual life coach is that guide who helps you come to terms with your deep desires; those that narrow down to your purpose in life. The minute you identify that purpose you become one happy person; waking up each morning with optimism and knowing you have a valuable task ahead. Being able delve within you in a spiritual way, of course, makes you realize the uniqueness of your purpose because nobody else can accomplish what you were born to do. If that realization does not get you motivated straightaway, you surely cannot bet on anything else on earth to do that.

To help you formulate a doable plan of action

How many times have you wished to do something but ended up a non-starter? Sometimes that happens because you feel overwhelmed or because you let doubts get the better of you. Such are the hindrances which your coach helps you overcome by drawing out a specific plan for you. And when that particular plan is ready for implementation, your spiritual life coach shows you how to mark success along the way and to keep the fire burning.

To uproot the obstacles that bar or slow down your progress

You may know what your mission in this life is. However, it is often a herculean task to get tangible plans running. And, in fact, it is usually not a matter of resources, but demons from your days of ignorance that deter your progress. The word *cannot* keeps cropping up in your mind; fears of ridicule rear their ugly head; self doubt sets in; and all these and other obstacles surface numbing you to inertia. However, your coach will know self doubt when it begins to eat into you and will figure out a plan of getting you back on focus.

Is a self help book not good enough?

Well, that one is not to be trashed. But if all you needed were books even in conventional education, who would ever go to school or hire a teacher? There is good reason people opt to go for a coach.

For starters, you need someone to be accountable to until such a time as you can walk your spiritual journey in your sleep – figuratively speaking.

You need someone who will design a workable plan for you. In fact, a good coach will not come with a set plan for you to fit in. Rather, it is your purpose and your uniqueness that will determine the kind of plan he or she ends up designing.

And what is the case for a self help book? Usually it will come with a set plan for you and everyone else – much like hospital garments. Nobody really looks great in them. Likewise, if you try to fit your desires within a generic plan, you are likely going to feel uncomfortable within no time and possibly give up.

A coach is usually on standby to answer your questions unlike a self help book which just serves you lots and lots of advice. Advice is good but you need to have someone to ensure you digest it and put it to good use. When it comes to periods of self doubt, your good coach is on standby to urge you on. So really, with a coach you are talking of learning on real time basis which ensures that you remain true to your cause.

Are you able to distinguish spiritual life coaching from common therapy?

Of course, these two may share something in that both therapy and spiritual life coaching help you get past your current and past hurt, but spiritual life coaching goes further to help you deal with your own future.

Specifically, this is what transpires along the lines of spiritual life coaching:

- You personally lay out your life as it is with the help of your coach

- You dismantle the patterns that have always kept you grounded and not pursuing your life purpose

- You remain on track once you have begun your route to success without succumbing to distractions and challenges

- Above all, a spiritual energy coach bases his or her guidance on the central law of the universe, which is that everything is actually energy. That law brings out the importance of respecting everything and everyone and working towards living in harmony with other beings.

Benefits of Spiritual Coaching

- Your intuition is heightened and you understand yourself far better than before. Subsequently, you can manage to get in touch with your innermost desires that bring out your life's purpose.

- You now notice opportunities that you would otherwise have been oblivious of.

- You are able to avoid obstacles that would otherwise have derailed you or slowed you down.

- You are able to create a good environment with positive energies boosting your willpower. You also find yourself attracting more support than opposition in all important aspects including availability of resources and people support.

- Your past inhibiting fears and doubts disappear and you cease to be your own enemy when it comes to taking initiative. Instead, you become self confident, taking every step with intent and purpose.

- Your life begins to shine with blessings as well as successes that you never knew before and repeat mistakes clear out of your life.

Using common examples, success in spirituality manifests itself in:

- A thriving business or even career when that is the route to fulfilling your purpose

- A fruitful and fulfilling romantic relationship in terms of a supportive soul mate who brings out your sensuality

- Excellent health both physically and psychologically, which makes you love whom you are and the way you look

- Enthusiasm in life which you can see from the motivation you have as you get up every morning

- Success in what you put your mind to within the path of realizing your life goals

- A can-do sort of attitude no matter your circumstances.

Chapter 12:
How to Boost Revenues by Coaching Your Sales Team

If you have got a good thing, it is going to sell with ease – is that your thinking? Well, you are not the only one with this kind of mindset, but no matter how many you are the reality is that you are way off. Who knows your product is great anyway? Where is your product and where do your target buyers reside? Are you trying to sell a luxury product or a basic commodity? And in that regard, are you within an affluent community or are you on the lower economic zone? Those particular factors as well as others happen to influence your success or lack of it in making sales.

Owing to these variables, salespeople too need a coach to show them a sustainable way forward.

What is a sales coach supposed to do?

Well, a sales coach will first of all seek to establish where you are having hiccups.

For instance:

- Are you one of those salespeople who assume too much about the market? And have you heard of something called due diligence and market survey? These are things that your coach will remind you of and show you how to gather reliable data to work with.

- Are you short of faith? As in, are you lacking in self belief? Just know that your potential customer can read doubts on your face if you harbor them; and they are not also going to have faith in your product or even in you as their salesperson.

- Are you short of sales skills or are your skills outdated or somewhat rugged? You must surely appreciate that a salesperson needs to be smooth in everything aspect – talk; demeanor; and such. As they say, image is everything.

- Are you doing too little in terms of activity? Now if you get too excited when you make a single sale, it implies that you are not about to strive to make another one soon. It is alright to give yourself a pat on the back once you make that sale, but that joy should be just enough to keep you motivated; not too much as to make you feel like you have attained your personal best performance.

- Are you using the most suitable sales strategy?

- What relationship have you been creating between you and your potential customers?

After establishing where your challenges lie, your coach is going to help you move from where you are today to a point where you will have utilized your full potential.

Areas of Focus for the Sales Coach

How good is each salesperson in communicating with potential customers?

Style matters. It may make the difference between making a sale and being literally chased away from the neighborhood. You see, much as politeness is expected, you should guard against patronizing the people you are relating with. And being condescending is out. You cannot also approach potential buyers with an attitude of take it or leave it and expect to make much headway.

As a coach, therefore, it is important to demonstrate the right way of communication. How do you do that? Well, you can teach the salespeople the best way of framing questions in order to get helpful information. And remember you are not a lecturer. On the contrary, you are a guide who wants to leave your sales team with the ability to think critically on how to go about gathering information. So you could ask them:

- What is it you want to know from your prospective customer?

- What, then, are the questions that would provoke that person to offer that relevant information which you so much need?

This kind of approach to problem solving from the coach ensures that he or she has not dished out solutions but has rather engaged the salespeople in active thinking. Ultimately the salespeople themselves come up with the solutions. By answering Question b, your salespeople themselves will have managed to come up with the best way of communicating to their potential customers. Moreover, they will have done that with a positive attitude towards the whole coaching exercise. You may wish to summarize this point by saying you need to mind your own language and how you use it.

The individual needs

Coaching, as alluded to here earlier on, is an actual thought provoking exercise; a serious process that should leave the person being coached more thorough; more independent in problem solving; and more grounded. It is hence important for any coach to address the needs of every individual in the team, because it is obvious the team does not sell in chorus or in unison.

Each salesperson moves as a package and needs to be conversant with and comfortable in all aspects of sales. So, as the coach, strategize and know how to get to know each client in terms of:

- Each person's values

- Each person's passions

- Each person's strengths

- What standards the person maintains

- What boundaries has the individual set for protecting himself or herself

- The level of the person's integrity

- What the person's goals are

- What the individual's fears are

- Whatever motivates the individual

- The opportunities for self improvement at the individual's disposal

Remember the coach has opportunity to make proposals to the top management at the end of the session on ways of helping the team in terms of resources, opportunities for growth and so on.

Matters of attitude

Do you concur that thoughts precede actions; and actually trigger or inhibit action? If, for instance, your attitude is that your sales manager knows little about sales since he or she spends lots of time in the office, you are likely to trash much of his or her instructions. You may not even give priority to memos issued from his or her office. What damage do you envisage here?

You do not, for instance, implement the action of informing customers in your area of jurisdiction that there is a 3-day discount period if that is what was contained in a memo you read a day too late. Consequently, as your teammates are being overwhelmed with orders, you are whiling your time away wondering what the heck is making people run around. In short, with a bad attitude, you can easily miss opportunities or even mess up relationships. As a coach, therefore, you have the most challenging task of changing negative attitudes; beliefs; mindsets; outlook; and even philosophy and assumptions.

Lessons learnt

Again, you are not a lecturer who hollers the hour long and departs; leaving the students to dig out whatever they did not grasp from the library. With you, it is your role to establish what your client has learnt from your coaching. If the client seems not to have changed in any positive way, it is your role still to find out the reason. Possibly you can recommend a few helpful measures for such a client.

Future strategies

After your interaction with the client, what is his or her plan in making changes for the better? And as the coach, in order to confidently say you have succeeded in your job, you need to see the client's strategy in improving:

- Customer service

- Managing key accounts

- Such other sales areas

When it comes to senior management, you need to know how they plan on improving:

- Business development

- Criterion for hiring salespeople

- Development of talent

- Support and encourage underperformers

The client's energy level

You will not have done much as a coach if your client's level of motivation escapes your notice. It is the energy level that triggers enthusiasm that leads to being proactive. So you need to notice if that is high or low and also if it is improving in the course of your coaching or continuing to wane. This is very important because a team that reeks of apathy cannot make the organization any sales worth writing home about.

Helping your client acknowledge possible consequences

As much as coaching should not be seen as threatening even when carried out by the respective managers, there is a way you as the coach can lead your client, who may be your staff member, to see the possible repercussions of acting in a certain manner or keeping a certain attitude. That realization can itself be the ideal tool to trigger your client's change for the better. In short, you will be trying to make your client aware of the consequences of negative behavior.

So, since the unpalatable reality is that people have deep rooted beliefs and they tend to have an inborn tendency to resist something different coming from someone else, you may want to avoid too much critic and advice and instead throw in a few questions.

Sample questions you could apply in jogging your client's mind to self awareness:

- What number of customers do you imagine you will have by the end of the year if you continue relating with them like this?

- How do your teammates react to your way of working?

- What does your performance impact the department as a whole?

- What impact does your way of working have on your customers?

- How does spending a lot of time in the office impact your customers as opposed to being out in the field?

- How do you think this mindset you have is going to impact your career growth in this organization?

- If you insist on not changing the way you communicate with customers, what do you think will be the cost in terms of lost sales?

- If you insist on not changing the way you communicate with your colleagues, what do you think will be the cost in terms of support?

- How would you say the way you work impacts on your reputation?

- How would you like the organization to remember you when you are no longer an employee here?

Chapter 13:
The Benefits of Coaching to Executives

Why would an executive require coaching? With a salary of several digits plus luxurious perks, why would a CEO need a coach; and in any case being CEO is already the apex of the organizational structure? But Bill Gates, he of Microsoft, believes coaching is great for executives. Likewise Fred Wilson, the billionaire of Silicon Valley, thinks so too. Even Eric Schmidt, formerly Google CEO is unequivocally for executives being coached. What other assurance would you need if not from these very successful executives?

With proper coaching, the organization ceases to depend on routine performances and begin leaning more on realized talent. And it is true, if everyone within your organization managed to unleash their own potential, you might marvel at your returns. Do you then not see that by implication your marginal costs will be falling? How else do you think organizations begin to shine in their respective industries and progress is sustained? That is how it happens – everyone unleashing their potential.

What would a coach do for an executive?

- Guiding him or her in laying out a strategic plan for personal growth

- Helping the executive in reviewing existing company values with a view to giving them life

- Helping the executive in working out any interpersonal relations that may be strained and bringing stress in the work arena

- Guiding the executive in developing a more clear and decisive style of leadership

Results of Executive Coaching

- Rise in productivity within every sectors of your organization; accelerated promotions; and much greater profits

- Greater self awareness on the part of the executive. This means that the executive understands himself better and also knows how other people perceive him or her and appreciates the reason. The executive is also aware of the areas he or she needs to improve upon.

- Reduced bureaucracy and bottlenecks in implementation of decisions.

- A great opportunity for the executive to express his or her concerns; fears; expectations; and much more that a person holding a high office is unable to discuss with juniors or even fellow colleagues. In the process, the coaching period accords him a chance to gain a different perspective to issues, courtesy of the coach.

- Recognition of weaknesses and challenges. For instance, it may dawn on the executive in the course of in-depth interaction with the coach that the executive's beliefs and attitudes have been coming in the way of progress in the company.

- More self confidence in taking necessary radical action

- More clarity on the values the executive holds. This means there is no longer room for self doubt in giving the organization direction because the executive is clear on what his or her convictions are.

- A feeling of having been supported emotionally and in an empathetic manner. Many leaders at the top hardly get that and loneliness can really set in.

- A chance to hear blatant truth

  It is obvious that many people will not dare tell it as it is to the boss even when they can smell danger looming from his or her actions. Call it a tendency to bootlick; cowardice; or whatever you may – but it does no good for the leadership. However, during the coaching period, the coach bares the chilling truth before the executive.

- Improved skills in communication; conflict management; delegation; art of persuasion; and such other basic skills that keep the organization running smoothly and efficiently.

Chapter 14:
Summarized Tips for Coaches

Can a good student succeed if the teacher's style is wanting? No – the main reason this particular guide s laying out some tips that are helpful to coaches of all calibers.

Guiding Principles for Coaches

A coach should have the spirit for the job

You will find it difficult to succeed as a coach if you take it strictly as an hourly job that you cannot touch before or after hours. If you have noticed, many great coaches have a parental or brotherly spirit. They mind what their clients are up to in every sphere of life. That not only creates a bond of respect but also makes the client feel accountable, a big ingredient for success. And in this spirit of minding the welfare of the client as a whole, the coach avails himself or herself, at least by wireless, for support and encouragement, and also for quick unscheduled consultation.

Believing in a client's ability to unleash hidden potential

In other words, you are not a good coach just because you are able to refine a client who is already well performing, but because you are able to change the attitude of an ordinary client to a positive one and have him or her motivated enough to bring out talent not known before.

Getting satisfaction from helping others succeed

The spirit of giving and sacrificing for the sake of the client is necessary. As such, the coach cannot watch as the client falls off track only to point out the indiscipline or other weakness later. Rather, he or she tries to ascertain the client succeeds whatever the challenges.

Bringing out the client's best and allowing them to take lead

This essentially means that the coach is showing his or her trust in your abilities, which in turn boosts your self confidence and encourages you to take initiative. Similarly, when your coach observes this principle, as the client you get accustomed to thinking of how to circumvent problems while tackling other challenges to the best of your ability. In due course, that atmosphere makes you develop a good level of independence, which is what the coach would want for you ultimately.

Trying to influence the client rather than push and dictate

The relationship between a coach and the client needs to be friendly and not just one of respect. And that can only happen if the client feels valued and respected in terms of having his or her opinions heard. Lack of such mutual understanding can lead to a strained relationship which is doomed to yield very little in terms of coaching success.

Thriving on challenges and ability to adjust

A coach needs to be flexible and adaptable to circumstances affecting the client. Supposing the client had a part-time job but has now acquired a full time job – is the coach going to freeze and begin to look for the exit clause in the contract? On the contrary, the coach would be expected to work out a convenient schedule with the client under the new circumstances.

Continuous self development

You are going to remain a great coach who is confident of his or her efficiency in delivering results if only you keep learning and improving your skills. There are seminars and workshops; newsletters; and also other coaches that you can rely on to better yourself and keep yourself challenged. In the process, you are able to keep your skills sharpened and love for your job enhanced.

How to Build a Relaxed Relationship of Trust

As already mentioned here before, trust between the coach and the client is vital if the coaching process is to be successful. Communication also needs to be easy and not strained. How do you cultivate that atmosphere as a coach?

- By maintaining sincere communication that builds rapport between the two of you

- By having a good sense of humor

- By being sincere in your caring for the client

- By practicing integrity in the way you handle your client and his or her affairs

Why You Should Mind Your Questions as a Coach

Are we saying that some inquiries are out of bounds? No, not inquiries, but the manner of making them. It is understandable that you should ask your client questions. In fact, asking questions is encouraged because it is only after extracting information that the client had not volunteered before that you can know how to proceed with your coaching.

- Ask questions that excite your client in a good way and those that are likely to leave you both inspired

- Ask questions that make the client feel empowered and valued

- Shelve any questions that you think may come across as judgmental

- Avoid questions that ultimately sound like a roundabout way of dishing out advice

- Go for powerful questions as they are geared towards eliciting deep thinking and powerful answers or solutions. Of course, such questions reflect curiosity in an explicit manner.

- Your questions need to reflect empathy for your client's situation as much as they are meant to show curiosity.

- Make good use of your intuition

One reason you are considered a good coach is that you know how to make sound judgment. So in this regard:

- Know when to listen attentively to your client without offering advice

- Train yourself to always be present when communicating with your client. Your client can tell when you are half attentive and it does not do any good to your relationship

- Suppress the temptation to jump to conclusions prematurely

- Have an open mind. It helps keep biases and prejudices out of your work

- Use your intuition to decide what to say and when to say it.

Note

As a good coach, you are already aware that some issues cannot be resolved by mere coaching. If you identify such cases in the course of your engagement, point them out to the parties concerned and recommend appropriate action. In fact, in case you notice your client needs therapy, point it out as best as you can, letting your client know why the coaching will only be beneficial after the therapy. Likewise, if professional consultancy is required, point it out too.

There is a tool for each job and trying to force your coaching tool to help someone suffering, say, depression, cannot get you far. In some African culture they aptly describe such an attempt as trying to grind water with mortar and pestle – what futility of effort!

Conclusion

Now that you understand what the Coaching Questions are all about, you can begin framing your guiding questions accordingly. You want a situation where the person you are questioning feels comfortable to tell you anything, and also to frankly tell you when they would rather they withheld some information from you. In other words, you would like your questions to bring out the true thinking of your trainee or the person you have taken charge of. As you know, the more you understand your subject the better you are able to help them in their pursuit for success. And, obviously, the better they perform under your care, the more confidence they have in you. As nature would have it, the vicious cycle continues; because the more confidence a person has in you, the more they are likely to heed your suggestions. And so, implementing the skills you have learnt in this book can positively transform your coaching career.

The next step is to go back over the book as needed as you evaluate the needs of the people you are coaching. You can then begin to design coaching questions appropriately, depending on how much you know each of those people under your charge. As you abandon the old questioning style and embrace the coaching style shown in this book, you will find your subjects becoming happier in your interactions and enthusiastic about training and working. The power is in your hands. Make up your mind to implement the coaching style illustrated here, and don't forget to congratulate yourself for a job well done when all the people you have led are performing in the top league of their respective careers!

BONUS

CODEPENDENCY

How To Overcome Codependency And Develop Healthy Relationships For Life!

I. Madison

© 2015 Copyright.

Table of Contents

Introduction

Codependency: it's a pattern of behavior that affects an innumerable amount of people, yet, because it falls under the category of "dysfunctional relationships," it's rarely discussed openly. Nonetheless, those living in codependent relationships know that it can be extremely difficult to carry out daily activities and regain a healthy lifestyle. Furthermore, codependency in the U.S. contributes to an overwhelming majority of relationship issues. So, if you're part of a codependent relationship, you're not alone. The bad news about codependency is that codependent behaviors can worsen if the parties involved in the relationship refuse to receive treatment. On the upside, codependents *can* make a recovery and foster a healthy relationship moving forward.

This book will give you the knowledge and tools you'll need to move towards recovery from a codependent relationship. You'll learn how to spot the warning signs of codependency and identify the telling behaviors of codependent individuals. You'll also discover real, applicable methods of coping with codependency so that you can move forward and reestablish healthy relationships. This ebook will outline steps to get your life and relationship in a better place. Enjoy the book, and good luck in your journey toward achieving a healthy, rewarding, and fulfilling relationship.

Chapter 1:
What is Codependency?

Codependency is often defined as a type of behavior in which an individual becomes wholly reliant on another. He or she constantly seeks self-worth based upon another's approval. Oftentimes, one person supports the other individual's undesirable traits or behaviors. This can come in the form of addiction, poor mental health, underachievement, or general lack of self-worth or responsibility. Although codependency typically occurs within romantic relationships, it can also take place across other family dynamics, and can even be found in working, friendly, or community relationships.

In a codependent relationship, one individual seeks constant fulfillment from his or her partner. In some instances, both individuals can become codependent, meaning that both parties are dependent on the fulfillment provided by one another. While this definition in itself may not sound unhealthy, it's important to realize that codependents are problematic because they are unable to achieve a sense of self-worth on their own. They seek validation from others, and cannot establish autonomy by themselves.

Typically, one party in the codependent relationship makes great sacrifices in his or her life in order to put the other person's life first. The individual who routinely makes these sacrifices believes that he or she must continue to appease the other individual, since it has been ingrained in that person's mind that self-worth can be found only through others. This is unhealthy behavior, and can cause serious implications for both parties' mental wellbeing if left untreated.

In many instances, codependents are individuals who tend to support the unhealthy behaviors of their partners. For instance, individuals who pair up with people suffering from borderline personality disorder may be more likely to become codependents. That's because there's a great chance that they'll feel forced to enter into the role of caretaker, which fosters a sense of dependency. The caretaker relies on the sense of validation he or she experiences in being needed by another, and treats the individual who has borderline personality disorder with priority instead of focusing on his or her own life.

Codependents are also commonly partners of narcissists. Sometimes, the codependents in these relationships are referred to as co-narcissists. Narcissists often actively seek and attract individuals that are inclined to putting others' needs before their own. While the codependent relies on making others feel important to achieve a sense of self-worth, the narcissist thrives on that very feeling of importance, which is why codependency is so common within relationships in which narcissists are involved.

As previously mentioned, dysfunctional family relationships are also a different variation of codependency. While children generally must rely on their parents due to the limitations presented by their young age, dysfunctional families flip the roles of the dependents. In other words, children begin to monitor their parents' needs and behaviors. This is typically a result of a parent's (or both parents') unhealthy or destructive behavior towards his or her child.

A parent must take care of him or herself mentally and physically in order to properly care for a child. If he or she is incapable of doing so, a dysfunctional family environment typically arises. The child may become shamed, ignored, or have his or her physical and emotional needs negated by his or her codependent parent. Unfortunately, this scenario usually leads to the passing on of codependent behavior from parent to child, and the child becomes more likely to wind up in a codependent relationship as an adult.

Addiction is also a common source of codependency. Sometimes, one party in the relationship will become an enabler, and the addict's behavior is able to be continued partially due to the fact that the codependent acts in a way that allows it to persist. This is especially common in relationships in which one party is suffering from alcoholism.

While codependency is unfavorable and can be mentally and emotionally taxing on the parties involved, it is something that, once identified, can be treated. Next, we'll examine the signs and symptoms of codependency.

Chapter 2:
Signs of Codependency

One of the most difficult roadblocks in combatting codependency is denial. Oftentimes, one or both parties involved in a codependent relationship will have difficulty recognizing, and then admitting, the fact that the relationship has become unhealthy. Sometimes, an outside party or an intervention is required in order for codependents to recognize the issue. Moreover, there are instances in which codependents are fully aware of the unhealthiness in the relationship, but he or she is reluctant to outwardly acknowledge the issue or take action.

Luckily, there are ways in which we can identify codependency, which is the first step towards overcoming it and achieving a healthy relationship.

Firstly, it's important to separate codependency from interdependence. Within interdependence, individuals involved in a relationship are only dependent on one another to a degree. For instance, in a family environment, one parent might rely on the other spouse to help pay bills or carry out routines to help with the children. Likewise, the other spouse contributes in other, meaningful ways. This does not mean that they are codependent, or that they are relying on one another to establish a sense of self-worth; in reality, they are individualistic yet can still approach the responsibilities of a family in a shared, healthy manner.

Here's one way to determine whether or not you might be in a codependent relationship: ask yourself whether or not you are frequently second-guessing your behaviors and actions. Or, you might simply be experiencing an ever-present, high level of anxiety. Individuals in a codependent relationship are frequently judging themselves, reflecting on what they should have done or said differently.

In essence, one of the most common effects of living in a codependent relationship is low self-esteem. Oftentimes, low self-esteem isn't as easy to identify as one may think. Individuals who strive for perfectionism may actually be suffering from low self-esteem; likewise, they may outwardly appear to be confident, but it could be a façade. Inwardly, people who are experiencing low self-esteem may be ridden with guilt and shame.

Also, codependents are often people-pleasers. They feel compelled, and perhaps even responsible, for contributing to another's happiness. Typically, these individuals are fearful of saying "no" and may even experience anxiety when presented with a situation or invitation they'd prefer to decline. In many instances, people-pleasers will say "yes" to something that they may not have wanted to agree to, but felt compelled and will instead put another's desires and needs in front of their own.

Furthermore, codependents may have difficulty establishing boundaries. They often internalize others' issues, feelings, thoughts, or needs, and establish an unhealthy sense of responsibility for their partner's sense of wellbeing. Nonetheless, some codependents may become withdrawn and actively draw up their boundaries, making it difficult for others to become close to them. In other instances, codependents might vary the behaviors in which they establish boundaries; sometimes they'll let their walls down, whereas other times they might be completely withdrawn.

Caretaking is another common behavior found in codependent relationships. Oftentimes, the caretaker puts the other party in front of his or her own needs. The caretaker feels obligated to help the other individual, and might even experience feelings of rejection if the other refuses help. Moreover, the caretaker might become obsessed with the notion that he or she can "fix" the other person in the relationship, even if that individual isn't trying to overcome whatever obstacles he or she is suffering from.

Another behavior that might indicate codependency is overreaction. While most individuals do react to others' thoughts and feelings, codependents might feel threatened by adverse opinions. Instead of brushing off differing views, the codependent might absorb the sentiment and start to believer it; or, he or she might react oppositely and become extremely defensive. Either way, too strong a reaction to what should be an insignificant comment might be a sign of codependency.

Codependents also typically seek a strong sense of control. They might seek control over the other individual in the relationship, or they might seek extreme control over one aspect of their own lives. For example, codependents might become addicts in one way or another; sometimes, they'll even become workaholics to take control over one aspect of their lives in totality. Caretakers and people-pleasers might even use these behaviors in order to take the aspect of control to the extreme, using their influence over others to manipulate them.

Furthermore, codependents may try to control the other person in the relationship by restricting his or her actions. The codependent may try to give orders to his or her partner. Conversely, codependents sometimes won't let their partners participate in certain activities or behaviors that make them feel threatened.

While codependents often intrude on others' space, this can also become a physical phenomenon as well. Observe your behavior, or that of those around you: does it seem as if you're always spilling, tripping, or just generally accident-prone? Perhaps you're infringing on someone else's personal space, or vice versa. Establishing personal boundaries, both physically and emotionally, is essential to having a healthy relationship.

In many instances, codependents rely on dysfunctional means of communication. They may not be able to present their thoughts or feelings in a healthy, clear manner. Moreover, a codependent may have difficulty determining what he or she is thinking in the first place. If you notice this behavior pattern in yourself, it might be an indication that something is wrong in your relationship. Or, if you notice that you're unwilling or afraid to be honest with your partner, this could be a sign of dysfunctional communication. For example, if your partner asks your opinion on something and you're afraid to be truthful, it could mean that the communication has become dishonest, which is most likely a result of the other party's manipulation.

This is often referred to as the "doormat" side of codependents. The codependent becomes literally unable to determine how he or she actually feels about a given subject, because he or she is so used to simply agreeing with others to appease them. Nonetheless, it's important to establish your own opinions and formulate thoughts on based on how *you* feel. Codependents become chameleons, as their views begin to blend in with everyone else's.

In addition, at least one codependent (or both) in a relationship is usually given very few opportunities to get a word in, especially during arguments. One person may exhibit cues indicating that he or she is impatient, and simply waiting for his or her turn to speak instead of actually listening. That person has already determined what he or she is going to say, regardless of what *your* point is. Thus, the conversation will most likely become an unhealthy, one-sided argument in which one person's opinions or views will get squashed by the other's, instead of both parties trying to reach some level of understanding or compromise.

Finally, if you're concerned that you or someone you know could be involved in a codependent situation, assess the general emotions of the potential codependent: Are there signs of shame or rejection present? If you're suspecting codependency within your own relationship, have you sunken into a state of depression, resentment, or hopelessness? Usually, one party may develop a sense of failure: you might begin to feel as though no matter what you do, it's never enough to make the other party satisfied. Eventually, you could become numb and withdrawn.

As we mentioned above, the promising factor here is that recognizing signs of codependency is the first step towards overcoming it. You or your loved one may not exhibit all of the signs listed above, but chances are that if you've noticed at least some of these indicators frequently enough to become concerned, you may be part of a codependent relationship. Next, we'll discuss how you can move forward and work towards achieving a healthier relationship.

Made in the USA
San Bernardino, CA
23 August 2015